Fingerplays and Rhymes

For Always and Sometimes

by
Terry Lynne Graham

Humanics Limited * Atlanta, Georgia

HUMANICS LIMITED
P.O. Box 7447
Atlanta, Georgia 30309

Second Printing, 1986

PRINTED IN THE UNITED STATES OF AMERICA

Illustrations by Linda Eibe and Chip Eibe, age 7
Typography by Daniel R. Bogdan
Cover Design by Ann Houston

Library of Congress Cataloging in Publication Data

Graham, Terry Lynne, 1949-
   Fingerplays and rhymes.

   Summary: A collection of short rhymes and finger games on topics including the seasons, self-concept, colors, dinosaurs, weather, and special days.

   1. Children's poetry, American.   2. Finger play.
[1. American poetry.   2. Finger play]   I. Title.
PS3557.R223F5 1984   811'.54   84-10937
ISBN 0-89334-083-9

Contents

To parents and teachers of young children who need a fingerplay or a rhyme to cover every unit, theme and occasion: this book was written for you.

And for all children:

You Light Up My Life

I like the way you've learned to learn.
I like the way you wait your turn.

I like the way you've begun to share.
I like the way you've grown to care.

You light up my life.

I like the way you make your plan.
And that you say, "I know I can!"

I like the way you sing and play.
And that you know you're Special,
    today and every day.

You light up my life.

I like the way you color and have learned
    to print your name.
In many ways you're different, and yet
    you're still the same.

You light up my life.

Little children who have come so far,
And still have far to go.

Can you see what you've done for me?
Yes, I think you know.

You light up my life.

— Terry Lynne Graham,
Teaching Children to Love Themselves

Introduction

Dear Parents and Teachers,

I used fingerplays and rhymes in my classroom when I first began teaching some fifteen years ago. I knew then how they delighted my young students with their rhythm, imagery, and often humorous nonsense. As children learn to express themselves, they experience a sense of power and confidence. They begin to take control of their lives. The rhymes I used enhanced language and vocabulary development and made the children proud of themselves when they were able to recite the rhymes from memory.

As I continued to learn about children, I saw many more values in the daily use of fingerplays and rhymes. Such wonderful teachers they proved to be! With little planning or preparation, I could teach shapes, colors, early number concepts, or spatial relationships. Finger dexterity, hand-eye coordination, and attention spans improved. Froebel said, "What a child imitates, he begins to understand." As children reflect in their play the different aspects of life, they begin to make sense of their own environment.

Our school days begin and end with rhymes. Children can be redirected and encouraged to participate through fingerplays. Your child doesn't like to pick up toys? Sing it, don't say it. Make it a rhyme, it's done in no time!

The longer I taught, the more rhymes I needed to cover units, themes, topics, and daily home or family situations. I began writing my own, and with the help of neighbors and friends who inspired me with their ideas, I created this book. May you use it to teach, to direct, to humor, and to delight young children.

Fondly,

Terry Lynne Graham

Dear Children,

Young children have been expressing themselves through fingerplays and rhymes for more than 200 years. You are just discovering the magic of language and have many thoughts and ideas inside of you to say. I hope that you will enjoy learning the rhymes in this book so that one day you will pass them on to your own children or students. You may not know the meaning of every word, or even be able to pronounce them all correctly, but when you learn rhymes at your age, they are filed in your special memory box. Someday you will pull a rhyme from that place in your memory and delight some child, as I hope this book has delighted you.

Letters are meant to be answered. I would like to know your feelings and to learn which rhymes or fingerplays you have enjoyed most. Please write to me, c/o Humanics Limited, P.O. Box 7447, Atlanta, Georgia 30309. I also want you to know how much I have enjoyed preparing this book for you. I have loved hearing the children in my classroom say my rhymes. I have encouraged them to write their own poetry, as I hope that you will. You can write your own book too, and if you do, please send me a copy!

Fondly,

Terry Lynne Graham

Chapter One

Bulletin Board Brighteners

Bulletin boards can be more than pictures cut from magazines or fancy borders made of lace. Children should have a part in every bulletin board's creation. They can participate in the planning of the board, as well as through their art or academic work. Young children can decide where materials should be placed and what themes are to be represented.

Rhymes help the board to be more than just another pretty *place*! It becomes a teaching/learning tool. Older children copy the rhymes each month and make their own book of poems. Preschoolers will learn the rhymes quickly and amaze you when in June, they can still remember the rhyme for September!

BOOKS TO READ:

Chicken Soup With Rice — A Book of Months, Maurice Sendak.
Song of Seasons, Robert Welber.

September

Summertime thoughts, we'll remember,
Say "Hello" to new school friends,
"Hello" to September.

October

Leaves now turning red and gold.
Days are shorter, nights are cold.
Ghost and goblin stories told—
Happy Haunting! Here's October!

November

Crisp, clear days,
Or smoky autumn haze;
Give thanks and praise,
It's November!

December

Holiday merriment everywhere,
Secrets floating in the air;
Shopping lists too long to remember:
We're glad for that special month of December!

January

Snow and ice,
Ice and snow;
When you melt,
Where do you go?

February

The shortest month in all the year,
February at last is here!

March

Fickle month,
To you we sing:
Are you winter or
Are you spring?

April

Wake up, tiny seedlings,
Wake up, sleepy roots.
Let's get our umbrellas,
Let's put on our boots.

Here comes rainy April;
Her showers bring on May.
Welcome, balmy April:
We hope you're here to stay!

May

Hurray! Hurray! It's the first of May!
Outdoor fun starts today!

(for rainy days)
Hurray! Hurray! It's the first of May!
Inside our classroom we must stay!

(Hint: Substitute 2nd, 3rd, 4th of May, as you
repeat the rhyme daily.)

12

June

It's June, it's June!
Summer will be here soon!

July

Hot summer days—
No homework, no school.
I'll dangle my toes
In my wading pool!

August

In August
I must
Get relief
From the heat,
And a choc-o-late ice cream cone
Cannot be beat!

13

Chapter Two

Bringing Children Together
Making Transitions

Daily routines in early childhood classrooms are divided into blocks of time that vary in length from five to thirty or forty-five minutes. So children must move from one activity to another many times each day, and making the change can be difficult for young children. Giving them a cue such as ringing a bell, singing a song, or saying a rhyme, helps children to accept the changes.

Children need to wiggle and squirm before they are ready to listen. Give them opportunities, through fingerplays and rhymes, and your lessons will proceed with fewer interruptions.

Getting Ready

Let your hands go CLAP! CLAP! CLAP!
Now fold them quietly in your lap.
Nod your head now, one, two, three!
All eyes look right here at me.

Let your fingers SNAP! SNAP! SNAP!
Let your feet go TAP! TAP! TAP!
Turn yourself around for me.
Now sit down so quietly!

Lift your arms up in the air.
Shake them, shake them, everywhere.
Jump up high. Bend down low.
Now fold your hands and sit just so.

Beginnings

Sit up tall. Smile this way. (Make a big smile.)
Now it's time to start our day.

Quiet Time

Close your eyes, open your eyes;
Touch your little ear.
Open your eyes, close your eyes;
"Quiet Time" is here.

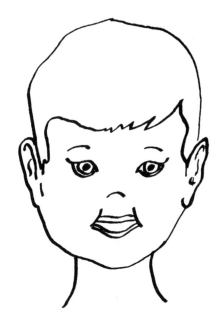

Planning Time

A time to smile. A time to plan.
A time to say, "I know I can!"

Recall Time

It's recall time! It's recall time!
We put our toys away.
It's recall time! It's recall time!
What did you do today?

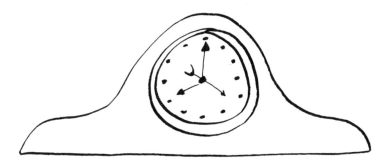

17

My Weather Window

Look out the window, what do you see?
Tell us all what today's weather will be.

I looked out the window
And I saw the sun.
Playing outside
Will surely be fun.

I looked out the window
And I saw rain showers.
But I know that's good
For the plants and flowers.

I looked out the window,
I didn't see the sun.
But on a cloudy day,
You can still have fun.

I looked out the window
There's snow falling down!
It's covering the houses,
The bushes, the town.

I looked out the window,
There's a chill in the air.
That's a sure sign of winter,
Frost's everywhere.

I looked out the window,
Is it rain? Is it snow?
Rain and snow mixed together
Is called sleet, you know.

I looked out the window,
But I couldn't see.
It wasn't too dark,
Just very foggy.

I looked out the window,
The clouds moved in the sky.
The trees and leaves are blowing,
The wind is passing by.

The Days of the Week

Sunday, Monday, Tuesday, CLAP! Wednesday,
Thursday, SNAP! SNAP! SNAP! Friday, HOP!
Saturday, STOP! Turn around and spin like
a top. Seven days in the week, you see.
(hold up 7 fingers)
Now we'll sit so quietly.

(Hint: Poem may be sung to the tune of "Twinkle,
Twinkle, Little Star.")

Circle Time

Here we are together, ready to start our day.
Let's make a magic circle, and hear what
    you have to say.
We'll talk about the weather and recite a
    nursery rhyme.
We'll share our thoughts and feelings,
Together at "Circle Time."

Tricks

Wiggle your fingers,
Wiggle your nose,
Touch your elbows,
Count your toes —
1 - 2 - 3 - 4 - 5 -,
6 - 7 - 8 - 9 - 10.
Now that you've rested,
Let's do it all again.   (repeat action)

Stretches

Stretch your arms out to the side.
Now behind you they must hide.
Stretch yourself up to the sky.
New pretend that you can fly.
Clap your hands and sit right down.
Careful! Did you make a sound?

Husha Bird

My teacher has a puppet she calls the "Husha Bird,"
And when she puts it on her hand,
We never say a word!
For "Husha Bird only appears
When we've made too much noise.
So it we know what's good for us,
We'll be quiet girls and boys!

(Hint: Use a finger puppet — Husha Bird, Husha Dog —
that says nothing but brings order to the group just by its
appearance.)

Your Eyes

Open them! Close them!
Give a little wink.
Close them! Open them!
Now it's time to think.

Show and Tell

What did you do? And what did you see?
Won't you please tell all about it to me?
Where have you been and what did you see?
Won't you please share all your treasures with me?

Quiet Walkers

Walking down the hall,
Walking down the hall.
See how quiet we can be,
When we're walking down the hall.

Chapter Three

Seasonal Rhymes

We alert children to the passage of time through observing the seasons. What can you tell me about the Fall? Winter? Spring? Summer? When does your birthday come? Time is a very difficult concept to grasp, and the fingerplays and rhymes here provide some concrete images to help children begin to understand an abstract idea.

BOOKS TO READ

Seasons of Time, Yasuhide Kobashi
When Will It Snow?, Syd Hoff
Jenny's Birthday Party, Judith Wolman

Fall

Beginnings

New school—
New teacher—
New friends—
New books.
I feel new, too.
Do you?

First Day

Shiny, sharpened pencils,
Desks all in a row.
It's the first day of school and
I don't want to go.

A very different teacher,
With a strange sounding name.
I want my last year's teacher—
Things will never be the same!

I remember all the things we learned,
And all the things we made.
The truth is, if you want to know,
I'm really afraid.

Leaves

Five red leaves, five and no more. (hold up 5 fingers)
The caterpillar ate one, now there are four. (thumb down)
Four red leaves, that's easy to see.
Along came a rainstorm, now there are three. (index down)
Three red leaves, nothing much to do.
A big wind blew, now two! (middle down)
Two red leaves, that's now much fun.
I glued one on my paper (ring down)
Now there is one. (hold up pinky)
Hang on, pretty red leaf! Your branches won't break.
You're one less leaf for me to rake!

My Oak Tree

The oak tree just outside my door
Has its lovely leaves no more,
And now, I wonder, What's it for?
Not shade, nor home for birds to sing.
When leaves return, I'll welcome Spring!

25

Lucky Leaves

Yellow leaves tumbling, (move hands like falling leaves)
falling through the air; (repeat action)
Falling in my front yard,
Falling everywhere.
Oh, that I could catch one (grab one in the air)
Before it blows away!
A yellow leaf, caught in the air,
Will bring me luck, they say!

Raking Leaves

My poor back will surely break,
If one more leaf I have to rake!
Crusty, rusty brown leaves!
Dusty, blustery red leaves!
Crunching, bunching, scrunching
　beneath my feet.
In a pile of crispy leaves, I'll find
　a welcome seat!

Woodland Forest Friends

Squirrels scurry,
Rabbits hurry,
Ants hide
Food inside.
Woodland friends, everywhere,
For long winter
Must prepare.
And just in time
They pile away their stock—
All without benefit
Of calendar or clock!

Ten Red Apples

Here I have five apples. (hold up five fingers on right hand)
And here are five again. (hold up both hands)
How many apples altogether?
Why, five and five make ten!

The First Snow

Watching,

Hoping,

Sighting the first flake;

Watching,

Wondering:

What will I make?

A snowman, a fort?

Angels in the snow?

A thousand flakes are falling,

Let's go! Let's go!! Let's go!!!

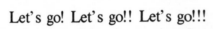

Five Fat Snowmen

Five fat snowmen were knocking at my door. (hold up five fingers)
This one melted, and then there were four. (thumb down)
Four fat snowmen were playing with me;
One more melted, and then there were three. (index down)
Three fat snowmen want to play with you,
But the next began to melt and that left two. (middle down)
Two fat snowmen, before the day was done,
Another one melted and then there was one! (ring down)
One fat snowman stayed out in the sun —
Silly, fat snowman! Now there are none! (pinky down)

Snowballs

Here's a snowball,

Here's a snowball!

A great big snowball I see.

Can you count them?

Are you ready?

One!

Two!

Three!

(Repeat action)

29

Snowfriend

Pack a snowball,

Make it round.

Roll it, roll it, along the ground.
Make one big ball, and one of middle size;
Then roll a smaller ball. Add a nose and eyes.
Give him a broom and a scarf of blue.
Now there's a friend to play with you! (point)

Melting Snowmen

Here's a snowman round and fat; (make circle with arms)
Out comes the sun and melts his hat. (touch head)
Here's a snowman with a scarf of red;
Out comes the sun and melts his head. (touch head)
Here's a snowman, fit as a fiddle;
Out comes the sun and melts his middle. (touch stomach)
Here's a snowman who waits for dawn;
Out comes the sun and he's all gone!

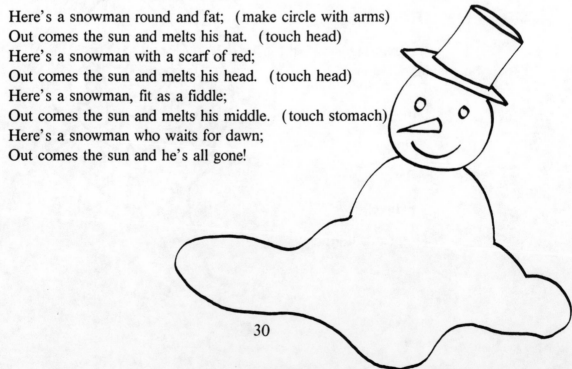

Merry Snowflakes

Merry little snowflakes falling to the ground, (fingers flutter like falling snow)
They're landing on the treetops, covering our town. (fingers flutter)
They softly fall on noses (touch nose)
And make our hair look white. (touch hair)
They seem to call, "Come out and play!" ("come here" motion)
As they fall throughout the night. (repeat first action)

Icicles

As I was playing all alone,
I made an icicle ice cream cone.
With an icicle cone you won't need a dish,
And you can have snow cones whenever you wish!

Ice Skating

Slip,

Slide,

A fast ride.

I can't wait,

Let's skate!

Sledding

High hills,

Spins, spills.

Winter thrills —

We're sledding!

Gliding, riding,

Slipping, sliding —

Flying, crying,

"We're sledding!"

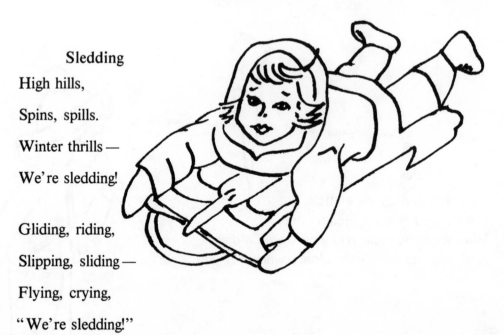

Mittens

I have three pairs of mittens:
Yellow, red, and blue.
If I ever lose a pair,
I will still have two.
But it never works that way,
That's not the way it's done.
I never seem to lose the *pair* —
All *I* lose is one!
And at the end of winter,
I have three mittens there:
One blue, one red, one yellow,
But not a single pair!

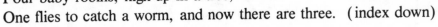

Spring Song

Frogs croak,
Rains soak.
Chicks peep,
Crickets leap.
Bees hum,
Robins come.
Birds sing,
It's Spring!

Baby Robins

Five baby robins watch Daddy Robin soar; (hold up five fingers)
One baby leaves the nest, and now there are four. (thumb down)

Four baby robins, high up in a tree;
One flies to catch a worm, and now there are three. (index down)

Three baby robins had nothing to do;
One tried his new-found wings, and then there were two. (ring down)

Two baby robins frolicked in the sun;
Another robin chased a bug, and then there was one. (ring down)

One baby robin, left all alone;
And this baby robin decided to stay home!

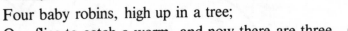

34

The Butterfly

He flies so high (thumbs hooked together, over head)
Then dips down low; (repeat action, hands at chest level)
He rests upon a flower. (hands on knees)
Only a second, then off again, (repeat first action)
You see, he gets paid by the hour!

Flutterby

If you ever watched a butterfly,
You would think the same:
To call him rather "Flutterby" —
Is more a fitting name.
For what he has to do with butter
I cannot understand.
But he can surely flutter better
Than any insect can!

Riddle

Soft as silk,
But won't drink milk.
Gray like fur,
But can't purr.
What am I?   (pussy willow!)

Tulips

Red tulips, yellow tulips, rainbow colors too.
You lift your heads
In my flower beds,
And say, "How do you do?"

The Crocus

Hello, tiny crocus,
Your arrival makes me sing.
I know you're pushing winter out
And making room for Spring!

Kites

Five bright kites I bought at the store. (hold up five fingers)
Along came a strong wind, and now I have four. (thumb down)
Four bright kites flying over the sea.
Along came a big wave, and now I have three. (index down)
Three bright kites, I'll give one to you.
Three bright kites, now I have two. (middle down)
Two bright kites flew too near to the sun.
Poor little kites! Now I have one. (ring down)
One bright kite — that's enough for me,
I'll keep it away from the kite-eating tree!

Skipping Stones

Down by the river where the water's deep,
I keep smooth stones piled up in a heap.
And when I'm feeling sad or alone,
I go down there and skip a stone.
I watch it glide and splash and sink.
It gives me time to stop and think.
And when this mood comes to an end,
I can get right up and start again.

Star Counter

Look up in the sky,
For Saturn or for Mars;
And did you ever try to count,
Try to count the stars?
I count from one right up to ten,
And then I must begin again.
It's not an easy job, you see:
So many of them, and only one of me!

Mosquito

He hums and he buzzes,
And on your arm he'll sit.
And just when you think that he's your friend,
You'll discover you've been bit!

Lightning Bugs

On a warm, calm, summer night,
You might see a yellow light
Dart in the air from bush to tree.
Whatever can that bright light be?
Go get a jar, with a lid that's tight,
And try to catch your own night light!

Picnics

Fried chicken, watermelon, apple pie;
Do you love picnics? So do I!

Lemonade, root beer, chocolate cake,
Lazy canoe rides along the lake.

Games and singing — let's square dance!
And don't forget, at picnics, you'll have   A   N   T   S!

Sprinkler

If there's a pool,
To keep you cool,
The sprinkler's spray
Is a very good way
To wet your feet
On a summer day.

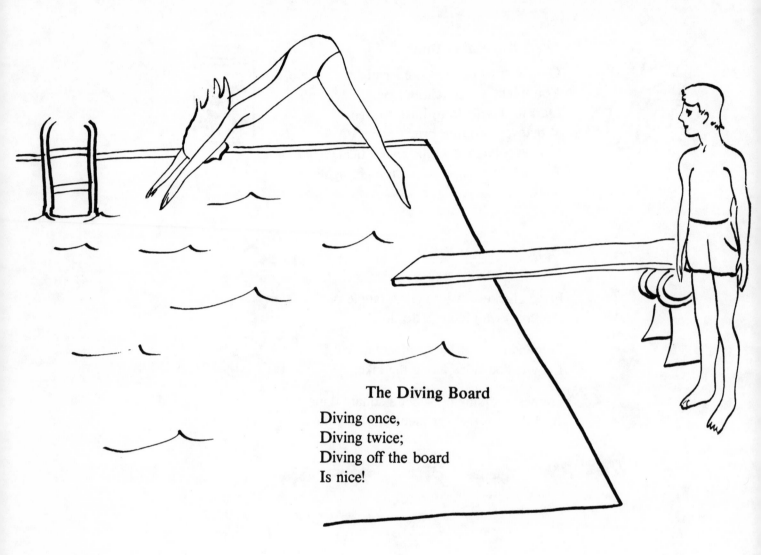

The Diving Board

Diving once,
Diving twice;
Diving off the board
Is nice!

Chapter Four

Self-Concept

Every child needs to know he is unique and special. There is no one in the world exactly like me! Children develop feelings about themselves through their interactions with parents, siblings, peers, and teachers. They develop positive feelings of self-esteem when they are encouraged, praised, and treated as worthy, capable individuals.

The self-concept often determines the success or failure of the child's school experience. Children who feel good about themselves take risks, meet challenges, and are more able to deal with problems. As the "significant others" in a child's life, we must take every opportunity to enhance and build the child's self-esteem in our homes and classrooms.

BOOKS TO READ

Who Am I?, June Behrens
I Like To Be Me, Barbara Belgeddes
I'm Glad I'm Me, Elbeda Stone
Leo The Late Bloomer, Robert Kraus

A Specialty

I am special,

As you can see.

'Cause no one looks or acts

Like me.

I am myself, one person,

ME.

And that's the way that

It should be!

Special Children

I like ___(girl's name)___, she's a special girl.

And she's her mommy's
And her daddy's little pearl!

I like ___(boy's name)___, he's a special boy.

And he's his mommy's
And his daddy's pride and joy!

I Am Special

I am Special! I am Special!
If you look, you will see,
Someone very special, someone very special,
Yes, it's Me! Yes, it's Me!

(Hint: Poem may be sung to the tune of
"Are You Sleeping.")

I Like You

I like you.
I like you.
I hope that you like me.

I like you.
I like you.
That's very plain to see!

I Am Me

"You're just like your mother, your brother, your dad."
When I hear that, it makes me mad!

I just want to act and look and be
One special person: I AM ME!

Feelings

How do you feel when you're happy?
How do you feel when you're sad?
What things make you feel angry?
What things make you feel glad?

Your feelings are meant for expression.
It's okay to laugh, cry, or shout.
Let your feelings come out in the open:
Let all those feelings come out!

Body Parts

Here are my eyes, they open and close. (point)
And here in the middle, that's called a nose. (point)
This is my ear, (point)
My cheek right here, (point)
My fingers together, (hold up hand)
My arms apart. (open arms)
But most important,
Here's my heart! (hands on heart)

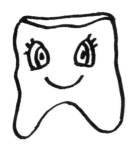

First Tooth Out

My first tooth came out today,
So tiny and so white.
Mom said the Tooth Fairy would come
While I slept that night.

But I was so excited,
I couldn't sleep a wink,
Yet, if I stayed awake all night,
What would the Tooth Fairy think?

And when I awoke next morning,
My tooth was gone, and yet,
How silly of me to even fear
The Tooth Fairy would forget!

I know she's very busy:
So many teeth, so little time,
And so I know I'll cherish
This special, shiny dime!

Freckles

Some kids, they call 'em "Speckles,"
Those spots upon my nose.
That really hurt my feelings.
They didn't mean to, I suppose.

But I'll try to ignore it.
I can, I will, I must!
Because Mom says my freckles
Are really fairy dust!

Freddy's Freckles

My freckles make me special,
    Special as can be.
Not everyone can have them,
    And mine belong to me.

They're sprinkled on my face,
    On my cheeks and nose.
I'll bet that I have freckles
    Upon my knees and toes.

My daddy says he likes 'em;
    He has them too, you see,
And in a crowd of children,
    He looks for freckles to find ME!

A Place to Think

When I'm feeling mad or low,
It's down behind the stairs I go.
And when I can smile and count to ten,
I'll come back up and start again!

When __(child's name)__'s mad or feeling low,

It's down behind the stairs he/she goes.
And when __(child's name)__ can smile and count to ten,

He/she comes back up and starts again!

Mirror Image

Look at my face.
What do you see?
Do you know anyone
Who looks just like me?

Your Birthday

Today is _____(name)_____'s birthday.

How old will he/she be?
Here are _____(name)_____'s candles,

Now count them all with me.
One, two, three, four!
And we wish her/him many more!

A Birthday Crown

On my birthday I will get
A birthday crown with my name, I bet.
My teacher makes one in a special way
To help us celebrate each birthday.

She makes it sparkle with glitter and glue,
And she writes in big letters
H A P P Y   B I R T H D A Y   T O   Y O U!!!!

Personal Wishes

Today is _____(child's name)_____'s birthday.

She'll have _____(child names kind of cake)_____ cake.

He'll she'll blow out ___(number)___ big candles,

And a special wish he'll/she'll make.
(child's name)_____ open all the presents,

One from every child here.
But the best gift is knowing
(child's name)_____ has grown another year!

Colors

"What color are you?" the small child said.
"Are you black or white or red?"

"Why do you ask?" his friend replied.
"Most important is what you're like inside."

Special Friends

I am special, so are you.
Did you know it? Yes, it's true.
We're both as special as we can be,
'Cause I like you and you like me!

Time Out!

I had to be "timed out" today.
I really don't know why.
I had to sit there quietly
And try hard not to cry.
All the children stared at me when
"Time out!" my teacher said.
I didn't cry a single tear,
But I know my face turned red!

New Shoes!

New shoes! New shoes!
Can't be beat!
New shoes give me
Magic feet!

At the Shoestore

We're going to the shoestore,
    There's so much there to see:
Sneakers, sandals, patent leather,
    All waiting there for me.
Shiny shoes in boxes,
    Wrapped in tissue, too.
Which ones shall I choose to buy,
    Black or brown or blue?

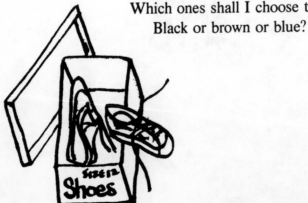

All By Myself

I can get dressed all by myself,
And I think that I look neat.
But Mommy always says to me,
"Your shoes're on the wrong feet!"

How can they be the wrong feet?
They both belong to me.
They are the only feet I have,
And they sure look *right* to me!

Chapter Five

Family

Children learn and develop by imitating those closest to them, most often their own family. Parents are the child's first and most influential teachers. Children will enjoy these rhymes about families because they are about people, places, and things they have already experienced. Children need to know that the problems they have are also shared by others. New babies, working moms, death, and divorce are mentioned, so that children will not feel isolated when these situations arise. Teachers should encourage discussion after reading such rhymes.

BOOKS TO READ

Nobody Asked Me If I Wanted a Baby Sister, Martha Alexander
Mine, Yours, Ours, Burton Alpert
The Tenth Good Thing About Barney, Judith Viorst

My Family

Here is Daddy. (thumb)
Here is Mommy. (index)
Here I am for three. (pinky)
Together we're a family,
As happy as can be! (clap!)

My Puppy

My puppy has a doghouse,
   just outside my door.

He licks me when I pet him,
   and wags his tail for more.

He's always there beside me,
   no matter what I do.

My puppy is my special friend,
   and a family member too!

The New Baby

I used to be the "special one,"
Till baby sister came along.
Mom's busy changing diapers,
Feeding Baby and, you see,
She doesn't seem to have the time
She used to spend with me.
Sometimes it makes me angry,
Sometimes I want to cry.
My new job as big brother
Isn't easy, but I'll try!

Triplets

Mom said, "We're gonna have a baby."
   Dad said, "Twins, maybe?"
But no one said that it could be
   Triplets! Count 'em: one! two!! three!!!

My House

Here are the windows,
Here is the door.
Come on in, I'll show you more.
Here is the kitchen, the living room too.
A bathroom, three bedrooms, and a room for you!
An attic, a chimney, and a roof above.
And my house is a *home*,
'Cause it's filled with love!

Working Moms

My mommy has to work each day.
She used to stay with me and play.
But daddy said, "We need more money."
Mommy said, "Don't worry, Honey.
There'll be lots of time for you and me.
It's not love's amount, but the quality."

A Day with Dad

My dad works in an office downtown,
And when he's home, he works all around.
He cleans up dishes and that job's hard;
Then he rakes up leaves and mows the front yard.
But Dad always finds some time for me,
And that's what makes a family.

Divorce

I didn't understand at first
    why Daddy went away.
I thought that it must be my fault
    because he wouldn't stay.
Did he still love Mom and me?
    "Yes," he said, "Of course."
"Then," I said, "Explain to me:
    "What does it mean, 'divorce'?"

Mommy

When I woke up this morning,
   My Mom had gone away.
She didn't say goodbye to me,
   Or tell me where she'd stay.

Now who will fix my breakfast,
   And tuck me in at night?
"Don't worry, Son," my Daddy said,
   "We'll work it out all right."

Ode to Blue

Blue was hit by a car today.
Mom wouldn't let me see.
We put Blue in the ground today,
Behind the big pine tree.

If there's a special place for cats,
I know they have my Blue.
'Cause all around the old pine tree
The prettiest flowers grew.

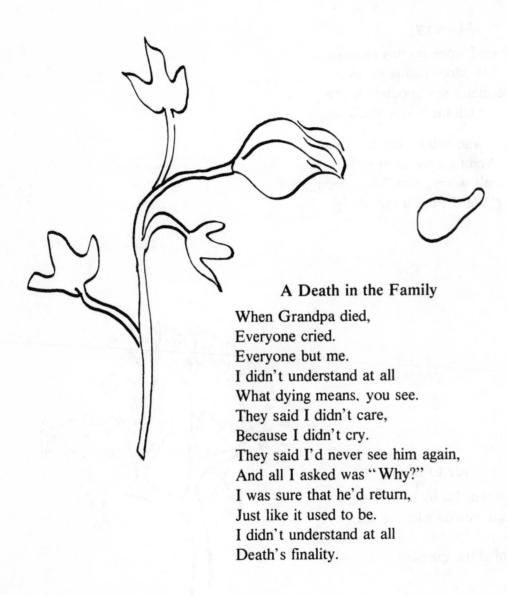

A Death in the Family

When Grandpa died,
Everyone cried.
Everyone but me.
I didn't understand at all
What dying means, you see.
They said I didn't care,
Because I didn't cry.
They said I'd never see him again,
And all I asked was "Why?"
I was sure that he'd return,
Just like it used to be.
I didn't understand at all
Death's finality.

Chapter Six

Community Helpers

Young children have always shown an interest in people they see working in their communities, especially those in uniforms! It is important to note that these rhymes show that jobs traditionally done by only one sex can be done well by either sex. Children who learn early that men and women can do the same jobs will have healthier, more realistic ideas about their own capabilities and aspirations. Of course, John can be a nurse and Mary can drive the mailtruck!

BOOKS TO READ

Mike Mulligan and His Steam Shovel, Virginia Lee Burton
William's Doll, Charlotte Zolotow
Postman Pig, Richard Scarry

The Policeman

There on the corner,
    in his suit of blue,
The neighborhood policeman
    is there to help you.
If you get lost,
    he knows what to do.
Just tell him your name
    and your address too!

Our Friend

The policeman has many jobs.
They never seem to end.
But this you must remember:
The policeman is your friend.

The Firefighter

This firefighter rings the bell. (thumb)
This firefighter holds the hose so well. (index)
This firefighter slides down to pole. (middle)
This firefighter chops a hole. (ring)
This firefighter climbs higher and higher. (pinky)
And all the firefighters put out the fire!

Mailman?

We watch for the mail truck to come down the street,
Then we run to the mailbox, eager to greet,
Our special mailperson.
And as you can see,
The one who brings *our* mail
Is a mail *lady*!

Helpers

This is Dr. Bell, who keeps us well. (thumb up)
This is Nurse Rick, who cares for the sick. (index up)
This is Dr. Heath, who cares for our teeth. (middle up)
This is Postman Dale, who delivers our mail. (ring up)
This one here — hey, that's me! (pinky up)
We all work together for our community!

Chapter Seven

Colors

We don't teach children about colors by saying, "Today we will learn RED." Colors are drawn to the attention of the children when we comment on Mike's *blue* shirt, the cloudy *gray* sky, or when we encourage choosing *purple* or *yellow* paint.

Color distinguishes objects: the *red* ball, not the *orange* ball. Color indicates the quality of an object: *Green* apples are not ripe. Learning to compare by color is an early stage in developing the skills of classification and comparison. The rhymes and fingerplays presented here help children to name colors and to become aware of color in the world around them.

BOOKS TO READ

Brown Is a Beautiful Color, Jean Carey Bond
What Color Am I?, Nye Loyal

Color Games

Colors, colors, everywhere.
RED right here, (point) BLUE right there. (point)
Point to a color, say its name.
Now you're playing the COLOR GAME!

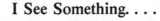

I See Something. . . .

I see something GREEN, do you?
Raise your hand if you see it too.

I see something YELLOW up high,
If you see it, wink your eye.

I see something RED as a rose.
If you see it, wiggle your nose.

Now *you* play the trick on me.
Can you find a color that *I* can't see?

Color Mix-Up

What would happen if grass were RED?
Or the sky were GREEN instead?
Could the sun be misty GRAY?
Would you like colors mixed up that way?

What if BLUE ducks couldn't quack?
And the WHITE house were BROWN or BLACK?
If color mix-up were up to you,
With a magic paint brush, what would YOU do?

Matching Colors

(Child's Name)   's wearing the color RED. (point to child)
(Child's Name)   's wearing the color BLUE.
I'm wearing   (Color Name)   and so are YOU!
 (point to a child with matching colors)

(Child's Name)   's wearing a PURPLE skirt.

(Child's Name)   's wearing a YELLOW shirt.
Are you wearing   (Color name)   that matches me?

Stand up now and let me see!

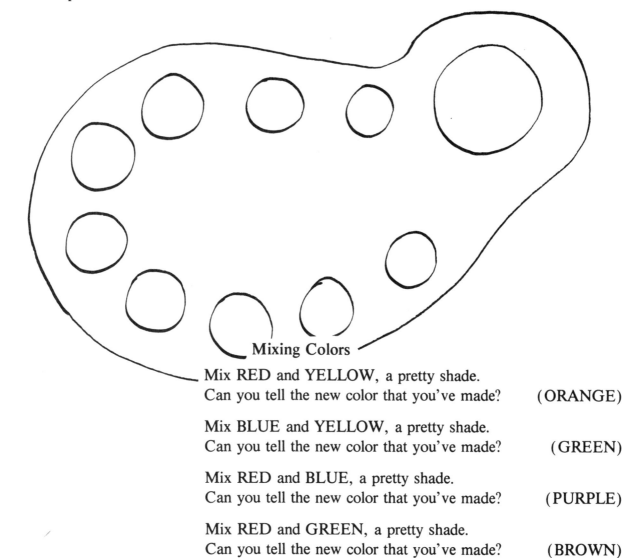

Mixing Colors

Mix RED and YELLOW, a pretty shade.
Can you tell the new color that you've made?   (ORANGE)

Mix BLUE and YELLOW, a pretty shade.
Can you tell the new color that you've made?   (GREEN)

Mix RED and BLUE, a pretty shade.
Can you tell the new color that you've made?   (PURPLE)

Mix RED and GREEN, a pretty shade.
Can you tell the new color that you've made?   (BROWN)

Colors

White is day and black is night.
Brown is pudding that tastes just right.
Green is the grass that tickles your toes.
Red is the color of the big clown's nose.
Blue is the sky on a summer's day.
Purple is jelly and yellow is hay.
Pink is the color of the rabbit's nose.
Orange is an orange, that's how it goes!
Now I've named my colors, as you can see.
Clap your hands if you're proud of me!

People Colors

People come in colors, as most things do.
But people don't come in green or blue.
What if people were striped or plaid?
Or what if you had a polka-dot Dad?
Wouldn't you still love him, for heaven's sake?
So what difference do people's colors make?

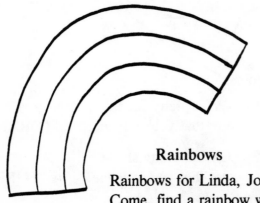

Rainbows

Rainbows for Linda, Joan, and Terry.
Come, find a rainbow with me.

Look for the gold at the rainbow's end.
And if you can't find it, make a wish with your friend.

For rainbows can come and too soon they're gone,
But a true friendship lasts all your life long.

Chapter Eight

Shapes and Space

As children draw squares, triangles, circles and rectangles in the air or make them with their fingers, they learn and reinforce the concepts of shape, size, and the position they occupy in space. Enumeration and directionality are also stressed in these rhymes, as well as imitation and following directions.

BOOKS TO READ

Shapes, Jeanne Bendick
The Sesame Street Book Of Shapes

The Circle

A circle, a circle,
Draw it round and fat. (use index finger to draw circle in the air)
A circle, a circle, (repeat action)
Draw it for a hat. (draw a circle in the air overhead)
A circle, a circle, (repeat action)
Draw it just for me. (draw in the air)
A circle, a circle, (draw in the air)
Now jump and count the three: One! Two!! Three!!!

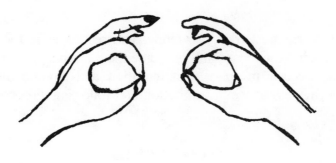

Circles Four

Draw a circle in the air.
Draw a small one, now compare.
Make one big; make one small;
Now draw a short one; now make one tall.

Rectangle

Here's a rectangle, straight and tall: (arms straight up, over head, fingers touch)
Two long sides, and that's not all.
Two short sides that face each other.
Draw one rectangle, now another. (draw in the air)

Triangle

Here's a triangle. (spread index and middle fingers apart; right index finger forms base)
Here's a triangle. (draw a small triangle in the air)
Now draw one more with me. (draw in the air)
Can you count them?
Are you ready? One! (repeat first action)
            Two! (repeat second action)
            Three! (repeat third action)

Hearts

Here's a heart. (bend index fingers to touch, thumbs touch, pointed down)
Here's a heart. (draw small heart in the air)
A great big heart I see. (arms high over head, hands touch, pointed down)
Please give one heart to me! (point to self)

69

Chapter Nine

Animals

Very often a child's speech centers on animals. "What does the doggie say?" Children love naming farm animals and imitating their sounds. The rhymes in this chapter were written to coincide with units about farm or zoo animals. When field trips accompany the study, the learning experience comes alive. Use the rhymes to introduce or follow up your units about animals.

BOOKS TO READ

The Friendly Animals, Louis Slobodkin
Brian Wildsmith's ABC's, Brian Wildsmith
In the Forest, Marie Hall Ets

Animal Rhymes

Cats purr,
To be sure.

Mice squeak,
To speak.

Horses neigh,
To say.

Hens cluck,
For luck.

Wolves howl,
And prowl.

Kids walk,
And talk!

The Friendly Duck

I met a duck along my way.
    She surprised me with a "Quack!"
I didn't know a duck could talk,
    So I didn't answer back.
She quacked again and nodded,
    In a friendly way;
And this time I answered,
    "Have a very nice day."

Baby Chicks

Five white eggs;
    One, two, three, four, five.
Five little taps:
    One, two, three, four, five.
How many chicks have come alive?
    One, two, three, four, five!

Barnyard Chatter
(Divide the class into two groups.)

Group 1: Who says "Cluck! Cluck!"?
Group 2: Hen says "Cluck! Cluck!"

Group 1: Who says "Quack! Quack!"?
Group 2: Duck says "Quack! Quack!"

All: Cluck! Cluck! Quack! Quack!

Group 1: Who says "Oink! Oink!"?
Group 2: Pig says "Oink! Oink!"

All: Cluck! Cluck! Quack! Quack! Oink! Oink!

Group 1: Who says "Moo! Moo!"?
Group 2: Cow says "Moo! Moo!"

All: Cluck! Cluck! Quack! Quack! Oink! Oink! Moo! Moo!

Group 1: Who says "Neigh! Neigh!"?
Group 2: Horse says "Neigh! Neigh!"

All: Cluck! Cluck! Quack! Quack! Oink! Oink! Moo! Moo!
    Neigh! Neigh!

Pretending

A pretty red roan
I'll give to you.
For me, a stallion black.
And we shall go a-riding
Upon our dreams and back.

The Colt

A baby colt in our barnyard
Tries to stand; it's very hard.
For he's just born, almost brand new.
Good thing for his four legs:
He'd never make it on just two!

How Now Brown Cows

This cow said, "My milk makes cheese." (thumb)
This cow said, "Butter if you please." (index)
This cow said, "Fresh milk for you." (middle)
But all this cow could say was "Moo!" (ring)

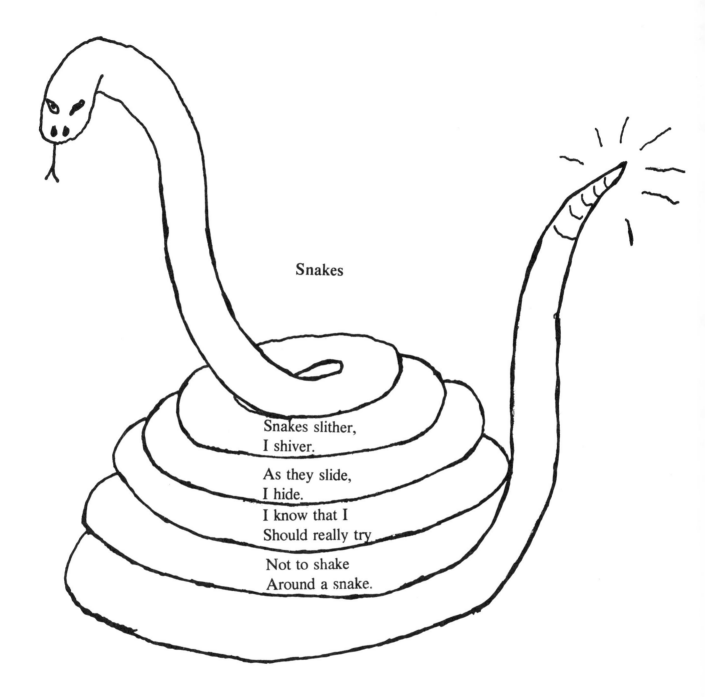

Snakes

Snakes slither,
I shiver.

As they slide,
I hide.

I know that I
Should really try

Not to shake
Around a snake.

The Monkey Family

Two little monkeys sittin' in a tree. (hold up two fingers on right hand)
Along came Mamma Monkey; that made three. (index finger on left hand)
Mamma Monkey said, "It's time to go!"
But the two little monkeys said, "No! No! No!" (shake finger)
Here comes Pappa Monkey, shakin' a stick,
And the two little monkeys sure ran home quick! (two fingers run behind back)

Tigers

Here's a Daddy tiger, (right thumb up)
And a Mommy tiger too. (left thumb up)
What do you call their babies? (wiggle fingers)
Why, you call them *tigers* too!

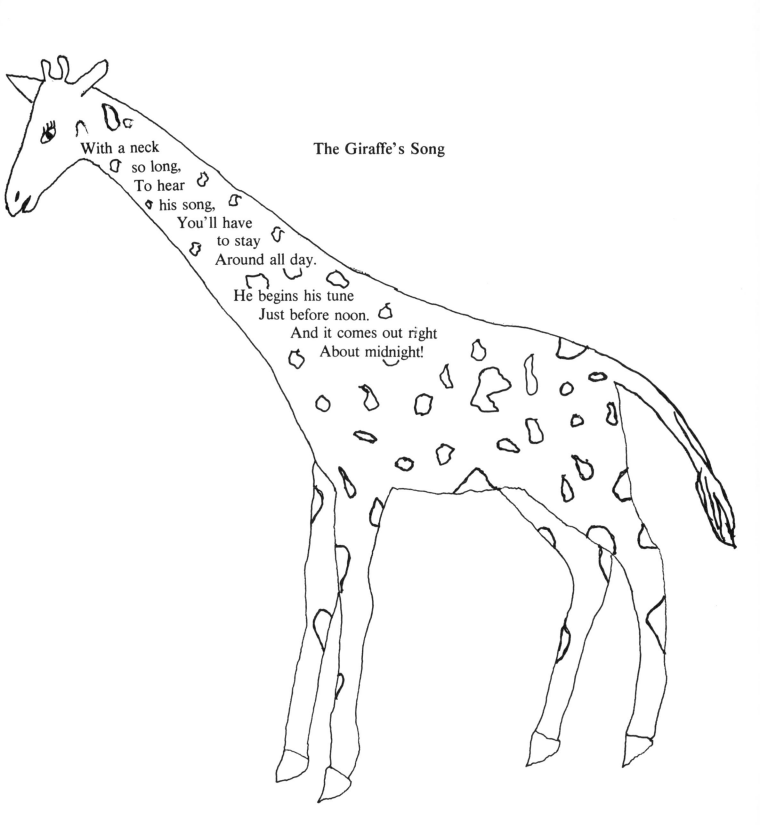

The Giraffe's Song

With a neck
so long,
To hear
his song,
You'll have
to stay
Around all day.

He begins his tune
Just before noon.
And it comes out right
About midnight!

77

Lions

Lions are just kitty cats, don't forget.
But would you want a lion
For a pet?

The Hippo

The hippo should really watch her weight.
   It's not healthy to be fat.
But could you get close enough to the hippo
   To try and tell her that?

The Elephant

If you should meet an elephant,
And say, "How do you do?"
Would you extend your hand to him,
And he his trunk to you?

For when you meet an elephant,
You must be so polite,
Because he's such a mighty beast
You'll want to treat him right!

The Zebra

Thank goodness for the zebra!
He's a special animal, you see;
For without the striped zebra,
What word would start with *Z*?

79

Chapter Ten

Dinosaurs

This topic excites and intrigues children. Learning about dinosaurs has motivated many children who were not interested in school at all. The art, music, dance, and learning center activities that accompany the rhymes in this chapter, will touch every aspect of the curriculum. Language arts, math, and reading all become fun when dinosaurs parade through the minds of your students.

BOOKS TO READ

The Rise and Fall of Dinosaurs, Anthony Ravielli
The Wonderful World of Prehistoric Animals, William Elgin Swinton

Three Great Dinosaurs

Brontosaurus, Stegosaurus, Tyrannosaurus, too,
Three great dinosaurs with nothing to do.
The three great dinosaurs went for a drink,
But before they got back they'd become extinct!

STEGOSAURUS

BRONTOSAURUS

Dinosaur Count

Dinosaurs, dinosaurs, how many do you see?
Dinosaurs, dinosaurs, count them with me.

One in the grass, (thumb)
One near the tree, (index)
One at the river, (middle)
And that makes three!

Dinosaurs, dinosaurs, how many do you see?
Dinosaurs, dinosaurs, count them with me!

Three at the river, (three fingers up)
One swims away. (index down)
Two dinosaurs (two fingers up)
Can stay and play.

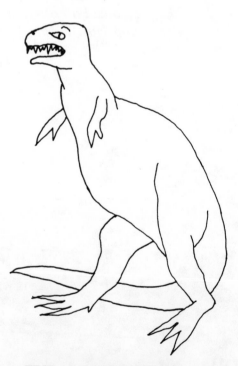

TYRANNOSAURUS

82

Dinosaur Walk

Dinosaurs walked like this (walk slowly, heavy movements)
And like that.
They're terribly big and terribly fat!
They have no fingers, but mighty big toes (point to toes)
And goodness gracious, how they grow!

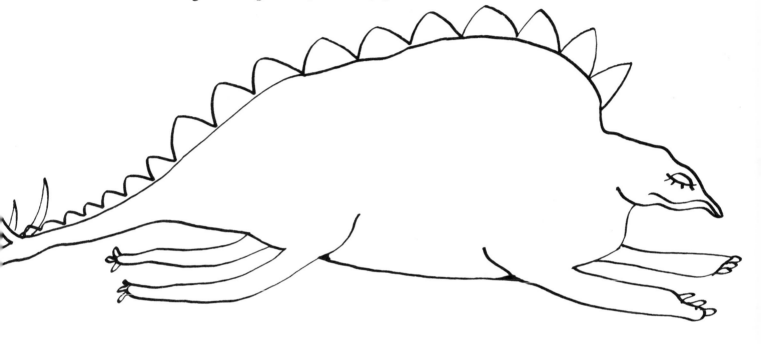

Dinosaurs Five

Five big dinosaurs, five and no more; (five fingers up)
One chased a butterfly and then there were four. (thumb down)
Four big dinosaurs, eating on a tree;
One went for a swim and then there were three. (index down)
Three big dinosaurs, didn't know what to do.
One went fishing and then there were two. (middle down)
Two big dinosaurs can still have fun,
But one went for dinner and that left one. (ring down)
One big dinosaur watched the setting sun.
He closed his sleepy eyes, and then there were none! (pinky down)

Chapter Eleven

Monsters

Young children experience fear about different things at different ages. They need to know that everyone is afraid at some time, and that *we* know that their fears are very real to them. Talking about monsters and portraying them as friendly, humorous, and at times, even fearful creatures, allows children to feel they are in control. Children enjoy being scared "a little bit." They love an occasional ghost story. We can help children to understand those things that they do not need to fear: loud noises, animals, the dark. We can also teach them to tell the difference between things that are real and that they need to be aware of, and of those things, like monsters, that are pretend and are for fun.

BOOKS TO READ

Lamont, the Lonely Monster, Dean Walley
Where the Wild Things Are, Maurice Sendak
Sometimes I'm Afraid, Jane Watson Werner
A Book of Scary Things, Paul Showers
My Mama Says There Aren't Any Zombies, Ghosts, Vampires, Creatures, Monsters, Fiends, Goblins or Things, Judith Viorst
Harry and the Terrible Whatzit, Dick Gackenbach

Monsters Everywhere

Monsters short, (lower hand)
Monsters tall, (raise hand)
Scary, (gnash teeth)
Friendly, (smile)
And that's not all!
Some are happy, (smile)
Some are sad. (pretend to cry)
Some are angry, (angry face)
Some are bad.
But we like monsters here and there.
We like monsters everywhere! (spread arms)

Monsters in My Room

Every night when I'm asleep,
Into my room the monsters creep.
I call to Mom, "Please come and stay,
"And don't forget the monster spray!"
She comes right in and sprays some here,
And all those monsters disappear!

Paper Monsters

There are monsters under the floor.
One has horns. I'll tell you more. (thumb)
This one's skin is black and green. (index)
This is the scariest one I've seen! (middle)

This one here has fish scales. (ring)
And this one here has claws for nails. (pinky)
By my monsters don't scare me!
They're only on paper for you to see!

Pet Monsters

If you have a monster,
You've got to treat him right.
Feed him and take care of him,
And turn on your night light.
For everyone thinks monsters
Are so very brave and strong,
But I know *my* pet monster
Likes the light on all night long!

87

Basement Creature

There's a Creature in the basement,
    And he's hiding on the stair.
Whenever Mom is gone away,
    You know he's waiting there.
He lurks behind the pickles,
    Just waiting there for you;
But if *you're* very quiet,
    You can scare him with a "BOO!"

(Hint: May be sung to the tune of the
Brownie Smile song, "I Have Something
in My Pocket.")

Alone at Night

When your parents are gone away,
    And you're alone at night,
Do you hear sounds when you
    Turn out the light?

Do you hear scratches at the
    Window and door?
Do you hear footsteps
    Across the floor?

Does the roof creak,
    The floor boards crack?
And do the sounds always stop
    When your parents come back?

Chapter Twelve

Nutrition and Health

These topics can be difficult to teach the very young, but they are so important. Children need to differentiate between foods that *taste good* and those foods that *are good* for you. Parents and teachers need to be reminded of good eating habits, too, so that we can instill proper nutrition in the children we care for.

Our nutrition unit emphasizes good breakfasts. We keep records of each child's breakfast foods and give awards for eating breakfast and for eating nutritious foods. We form a "Good Breakfast Club" and end our unit with a breakfast for parents, prepared by the children. Our parents are so pleased and many report their children are eating and enjoying breakfast. Some children insist that their parents share breakfast with them!

BOOKS TO READ

What Shall We Have for Breakfast?, Nathan Zimelman
Pancakes for Breakfast, Tomi DePaola

Vegetables

I always eat my vegetables,
Carrots and broccoli too.
My mother says they'll help me grow:
"Eat them, they're good for you!"
But there is just one vegetable
I can't seem to eat:
I don't care if I ever grow
If I have to eat a beet!

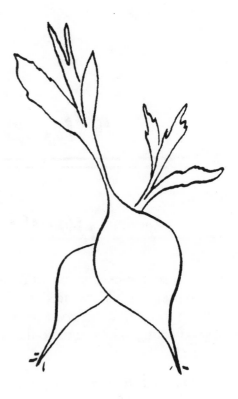

Good Foods

Mommy says to try some cheese;
Eat your spinach, if you please.
A glass of milk is good for you —
But shouldn't moms eat good foods, too?

Basic Food Groups

Here are the food groups:
Dairy, bread, and meat;
And don't forget that vegetables
Are important for you to eat.
Have a food from each food group
Each and every day,
And you'll grow strong and healthy —
Good nutrition is the way!

90

Snacks

Here's a big red apple, that's so good for me. (thumb)
Here's a crunchy carrot, nutritious as can be. (index)
Here's a stick of yellow cheese, I'll eat it on a break. (middle)
Here are nuts and raisins, a snack that I can make. (ring)
And here's a glass of cold milk, all good foods, you see. (pinky)
I'll stay away from junk foods, if I want to stay healthy!

Medicine

Medicine is for your parents
To give you when you're ill.
So never open medicine or take
Any kind of pill!

For medicine can help you,
But some kinds can make you sick.
Let Mom or Dad give the medicine,
If you're to get well quick!

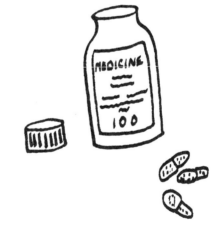

Going to Dr. Mott

"This isn't going to hurt you, "
Said friendly Dr. Mott.
That's easy for *him* to say,
When it's *me* getting the shot!

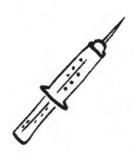

Daily Requirements

Brush your teeth
After every meal,
And you'll be surprised
At how good you feel!

Wash your face
Morning, noon, and night;
Add a smile,
And you'll look just right!

Take good care
Of your pretty hair;
Washed and combed
You'll look so fair!

Brush! Brush! Brush!

Here are my teeth, all shiny and bright. (point to teeth)
I brush them each morning,
I brush them at night. (brushing motion)
I visit my dentist, at least twice a year.
And that makes a healthy
Smile right here! (point)

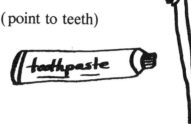

Bathtub Time

A rubber duck and a sailboat:
I watch my bath toys sink and float.
They keep me company in the tub
'Til Mommy makes me soap and scrub.
I love to take a bath each night,
And go to bed all clean and bright!

My Bath

Getting in the bathtub is so much fun, you see:
Ducks and trucks and sailboats
All waiting there for me.
I guide them through the bubbles,
Then put them in their place.
Then Mommy always asks me:
"Did you wash your face?"

Chapter Thirteen

The Sea

Do you know my friend the sea? Introduce your children to the beauty of the sea through these fingerplays and rhymes. The children will enjoy every aspect of this topic, from imagining what it would be like to ride a whale through the waves, to impressing their parents with pictures of a *sea anemone*. The rhymes stimulate thinking and reinforce facts about underwater life.

BOOKS TO READ

Fish Is Fish, Leo Lionni
Swimmy, Leo Lionni
Arty the Smarty, Faith McNulty

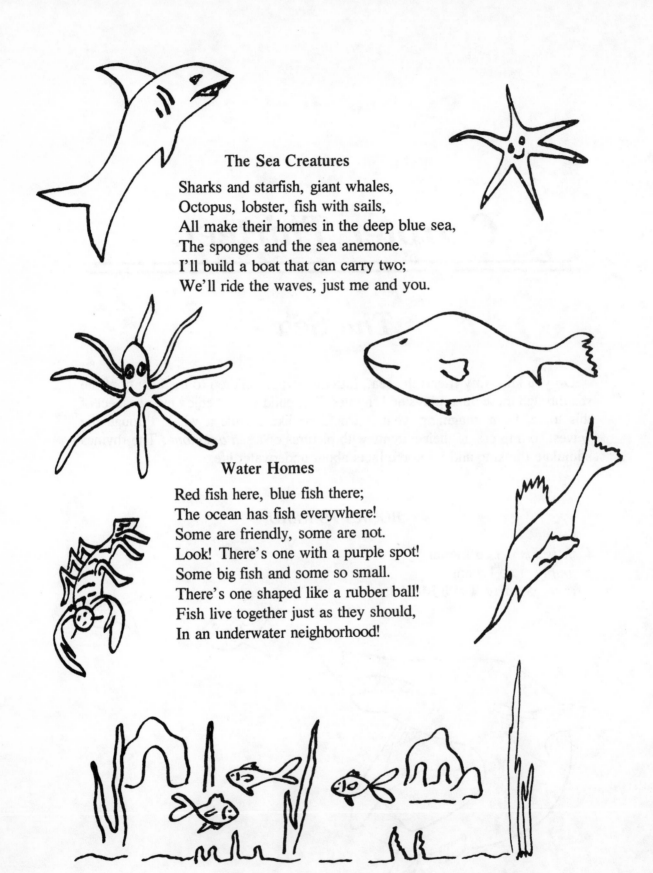

The Sea Creatures

Sharks and starfish, giant whales,
Octopus, lobster, fish with sails,
All make their homes in the deep blue sea,
The sponges and the sea anemone.
I'll build a boat that can carry two;
We'll ride the waves, just me and you.

Water Homes

Red fish here, blue fish there;
The ocean has fish everywhere!
Some are friendly, some are not.
Look! There's one with a purple spot!
Some big fish and some so small.
There's one shaped like a rubber ball!
Fish live together just as they should,
In an underwater neighborhood!

Swimming School

Did you know fish swim in schools?
In the ocean that's one of the rules.
There's safety in numbers, fish all know.
They stay together wherever they go.

Schools for Fish

In the Fish School, they don't learn
How to read or wait their turn;
And they don't learn one and one make two,
And they don't learn to paint or glue.
They never have to sit up straight,
Or be quiet or divide by eight.
They do pretty much just as they wish —
I think I'll join that school for fish!

My Whale

I want to ride a whale,
    Through the waves today.
If he'd be still and come ashore,
    I know that we could play.
I'd feed him lots of plankton,
    Then on his back I'd climb,
And I know that we'd together
    Have a whale of a time!

Save the Whale

If we aren't kind to whales,
 And help them to be free,
We'll only remember the whale
 By his lonely memory.

Hermit Crabs

I watch you run and hide all day,
And try to catch you as I play.
I want to take you home with me,
But I wonder: would you miss the sea?

Fish and the Fisherman

Three little fish were swimmin' in the brook: (hold up 3 fingers)
One little fish saw the fisherman's hook.
One quick look was all it took, and there were
Two little fish swimmin' in the brook. (2 fingers)
Two little fish were swimmin' in the brook;
One quick look was all it took, and there was
One little fish swimmin' in the brook. (one finger)
One little fish was swimmin' in the brook;
One quick look was all it took, and there were
No more fish swimmin' in the brook. (fist)
Then the fisherman said, "These fish are so small,
They won't be good for my dinner at all!"
Back in the brook— splash! ONE! TWO! THREE!
And now they're happy as they can be!

Shells

I found a seashell at the shore,
And held it to my ear.

I thought I heard the ocean roar,
As I held it near.

And now when I remember
My summer at the sea,

My seashell echoes back the sound
In pleasant memory.

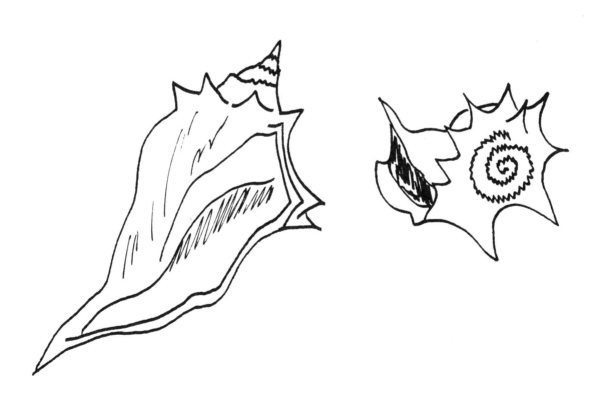

Chapter Fourteen

Teddy Bears

Everyone loves teddy bears! Art projects, such as teddy bears puppets and day/night pictures are incorporated into a week-long unit. A Teddy Bear Parade ends our week as we all come to school wearing our pajamas and hugging our favorite teddy bear or stuffed animal. Our math center has boxes of teddy bears cut from construction paper to count, and large teddy bears to hang on the easel. Bedtime stories end each day and here are some of our favorites:

BOOKS TO READ

Teddy Bears 1 to 10, Susanna Gretz
Bedtime for Frances, Russell Hoban
Goodnight Moon, Margaret Wise Brown
Corduroy, Don Freeman
The Day We Saw the Sun Come Up, Alice Goudey

My Teddy Bear

When I go to bed at night,
I hug my Teddy Bear;
And even though I'm fast asleep,
I know that he is there.
He watches me throughout the night,
And guards me as I sleep.
A better friend I'll never find —
My special friend to keep.

The Koala

He's like a little Teddy Bear,
In a eucalyptus tree.
He'd never be a pet, I guess:
He's used to being free.
He'll stay in Australia —
I know he likes it there.
So he'll be, as you'll see,
Mother Nature's Teddy Bear!

Teddy Bear Count

This little Teddy Bear goes to town; (thumb)
This Teddy Bear jumps up and down. (index)
This Teddy Bear nods his head; (middle)
This Teddy Bear butter his bread. (ring)
This little Teddy Bear sleeps with me; (pinky)
And he's as happy as he can be!

Teddy Bear! Teddy Bear!

Teddy Bear, Teddy Bear,
Nod your head. (nod head)
Teddy Bear, Teddy Bear,
Go to bed. (rest head on hands)
Teddy Bear, Teddy Bear,
Wink your eye. (wink)
Teddy Bear, Teddy Bear,
Jump so high. (jump)
Teddy Bear, Teddy Bear,
Touch your knee. (touch knee)
Teddy Bear, Teddy Bear,
Sit quietly. (sit down)

Chapter Fifteen

Transportation

Let's talk about "Things That Go!" and we'll help children learn classification and counting skills. What things go in the air? on land? in the water? Help the children to travel by means of their imaginations, and they'll always be "on the go."

Post some of the rhymes from this chapter in the block area to stimulate building airports and train roundhouses.

BOOKS TO READ

When I Go to the Moon, Claudia Lewis
Transportation of Tomorrow, Frank Ross
Highways across Waterways: Ferries, Bridges and Tunnels, Charles Gramet

Things That Go

Buses, planes, trucks, trains;
Cars blue, wagons too.
Monorails, boats with sails;
Army jeeps, old heaps;
Ships at sea;
And, of course, ME!

Traveling

Airplanes fly, with wings on high;
Ships sail, on a watery trail.
Cars are the way we travel most,
And they line highways coast to coast.

Wings

Silver ships, high in the air:
Airplanes take us everywhere.
They leave their trails
Of white jet streams,
And transport us
In and out of dreams.

Imagine

Imagine eating vegetables and meat
While cruising at thirty thousand feet!
Imagine watching clouds pass by,
As through the air you swiftly fly.
Imagine sleeping in the light,
And seeing day turn into night.
Yes, it's true, and you can bet
This all can happen on a jet!

Trains

This little train goes down the track; (pinky)
This little train goes up and back. (ring)
This little train goes round and round; (middle)
This little train makes a very loud sound. (index)
    Whoo! Whoo! (blow on thumb)

The Train

Here's the engine and the smoke stack;
Here's the station on the railroad track.
See the people stand and cheer,
For the proud train engineer.
Here's the whistle — ready, BLOW!
And the caboose follows wherever we go!

Homes

Planes live in hangars,
   Ships at the dock;
Trains in the roundhouse,
   New cars in the lot.

Twin Transport

The twins have a carriage that's built for two.
I think they think that's neat, don't you?
They seem to have double the fun
Than if the two had to ride as one!

Trucks

Trucks carry vegetables, chickens, and hogs;
Trucks carry furniture, cement, and logs.
Trucks can carry most anything:
What would you like this truck to bring?

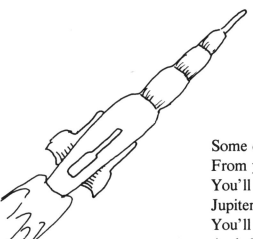

Rocket Ride

Some day you'll ride a rocket
From your house to the stars.
You'll make a stop at Venus,
Jupiter and Mars.
You'll take a ride 'round Saturn's rings,
And shop upon the moon.
You'll have to hurry up now
To make it home by noon!

Big Wheels

See our Big Wheels, all in a row.
The starter says, "Get ready, get set, go!"
Down the street and up the street,
Then down the street again.
Who has the fastest Big Wheel?
Let's see who will win!

What If. . . .

You should meet
A plane coming down your very own street?
A boat could fly
Up in the sky?
A bike could ride
Upon the tide?
You could walk
On a cloud somehow?
What kind of world
Would *that* be now?

Chapter Sixteen

Weather

One of a child's first scientific observations occurs when he notes the weather. Encourage children to report the weather and record daily changes. Graph the number of rainy days in April and compare them to the number of sunny days in May. Help children to make predictions and discuss apprehensions about thunder, lightning, and tornadoes. Many of the rhymes in this chapter were written to allay the fears children have concerning weather conditions that are not harmful to them, and to alert them to those that are.

BOOKS TO READ

Sometimes I'm Afraid, Jane Werner Watson
Why Can't You See the Wind?, Sally Cartwright
Thunderstorm, Thelma Harrington Bell
It Looked Like Spilt Milk, Charles G. Shaw

Wishful Thinking

When it's cold,
I wish for hot.

And when it's hot,
I wish it's not.

And when it rains,
I wish for sun.

Weather satisfies
No one!

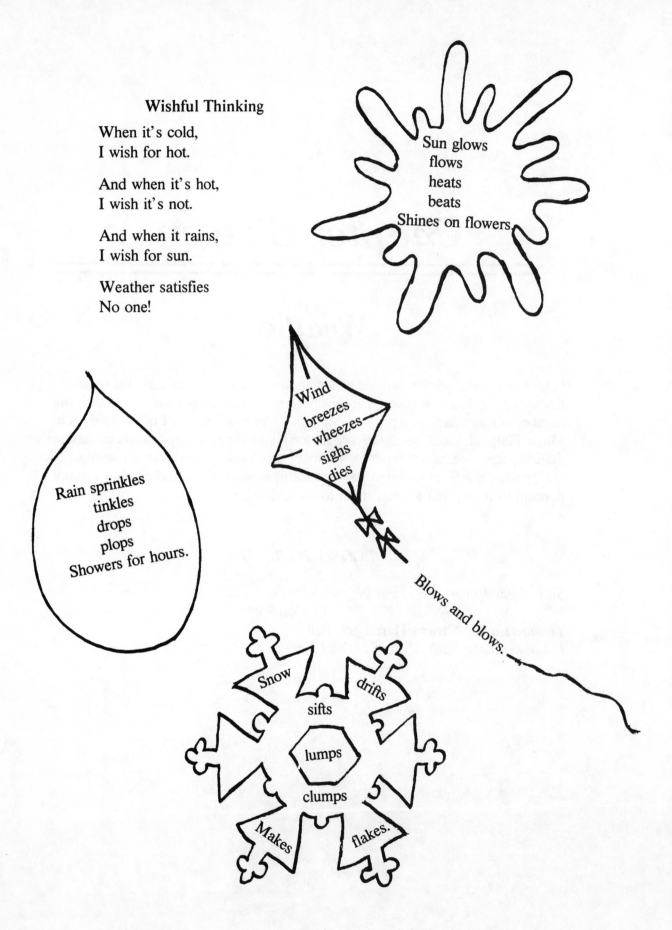

Sun glows
flows
heats
beats
Shines on flowers.

Wind
breezes
wheezes
sighs
dies

Blows and blows.

Rain sprinkles
tinkles
drops
plops
Showers for hours.

Snow drifts
sifts
lumps
clumps
Makes flakes.

Stormy Weather

Thunder boomers fill the air,
Lightning's striking everywhere.
Mom holds me close,
And strokes my hair,
Until the storm is over.

Rain

The rain makes puddles where it falls.
The bushes look like waterfalls.
And places where I used to play,
Look like rivers and lakes today!

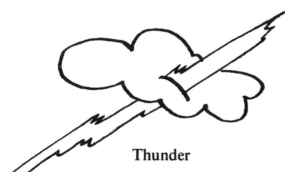

Thunder

Thunder crashes all around.
They tell me, "It's just a sound.
It can't hurt anyone, you see."
But I wonder if thunder's
Afraid of *me*?

Strange Weather

Hail the size of beach balls,
A foot of snow or two;
Hurricanes in Kansas—
What's this weather coming to?
A heat wave in Alaska;
Snow in sunny Spain;
Flooding in the desert;
Rain forests without rain.
Whatever the weather,
On this we'll agree:
Forecasting tomorrow's weather
Is an impossibility!

Clouds

Floating pictures in the sky—
Upon a cloud I'd like to fly,
And see the world from way on high.
Come, ride a cloud with me!

Watching Clouds

Are clouds as pillowy as they seem?
And do they taste like custard cream?
Or can you mold them just like clay,
Or ride on one for just a day?
As long as no one knows but you,
Clouds can do what you want them to!

Sad Clouds

The clouds are dark and angry.
They must be sad, it's true:
For when a cloud is crying,
The rains are falling through!

Chapter Seventeen

Special Days

The holiday rhymes in this chapter follow the calendar year, January through December. Special days require special rhymes that the children will remember into adulthood. Do you remember a rhyme you may have learned as a child that you can share with someone? Memorize some of these so that, at the drop of a hat, you can come up with a poem for a special day!

BOOKS TO READ

Around the Year, Tasha Tudor
Washington's Birthday, Don Bolognese
The Fourth of July Story, Alice Dalgleish
Holiday Round Up, Lucille Pannell and Frances Cavanaugh

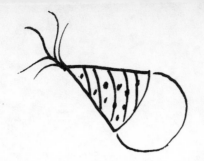

The New Year

The old year is over,
The new year's begun.
We'll hope for a year
Of good times and fun.

Bells Ring

Bells ring,
People sing.
All cheer,
Happy New Year!

The Birthday of Martin Luther King

We wish to remember you, Martin,
For all the fine things you have done.
You tried to unite the Black and White,
And bring us together as one.

Your deeds remain in our memories,
For what your stood for was good:
Love and peace among all people,
And the goals of true brotherhood.

George Washington

The first President of our country,
Your birthday we'll celebrate.
You had what it took to build a nation,
And to make a good country great.
Your honesty is remembered,
Along with your battles won.
We'll honor you on this, your birthday:
Happy Birthday, George Washington!

February Forecaster

Where is Mr. Groundhog?
It's February 2.
Come out, Mr. Groundhog,
We're waiting just for you!

Tell us, Mr. Groundhog:
More winter or soon spring?
Tell us, Mr. Groundhog:
What will your forecast bring?

The Groundhog's Shadow

The groundhog saw his shadow,
Then into his hole he drew.
If I saw six more weeks of winter,
That's just what I would do!

The Birthday of Abraham Lincoln

A country lawyer, strong and tall,
    A leader of our nation,
Your birthday gives a reason
    For a happy celebration!

Abe Lincoln

We honor you, Abe Lincoln,
Your wisdom made men free.
You wanted us to live in peace,
And share equality.

Counting Valentines

Here's a valentine.
Here's a valentine.
A great big valentine I see. (hands over head, pointed down)

Can you count them?
Are you ready?
One! (repeat first action)
Two! (repeat first action)
Three! (repeat second action)

A Valentine for You

I made a pretty valentine,
    With glitter, hearts, and glue.
And my pretty valentine
    I'm going to send to you! (point to someone)

Five Valentines

A valentine for mother, (thumb)
A valentine for Father, (index)
A valentine for Sister, (middle)
And little brother too. (ring)
I put one in the mail today,
Especially for you! (point)

Homemade Valentines

This valentine has lots of lace: (thumb)
This valentine has a funny face. (index)
This valentine is red and small; (middle)
This valentine is the biggest of all! (ring)
This valentine has glitter and glue,
And its message says, "I love you!" (pinky)

Handprint Valentine

Here are my little handprints,
   Especially for you.
They make a pretty valentine,
And say, "I love you too!"
(Hint: Have children paste a valentine heart on construction paper. Use tempera paints to make their handprints. Send this valentine to their parents.)

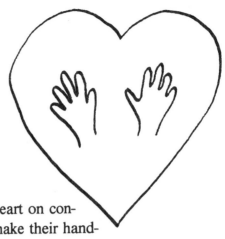

Butterfly Valentine

"Two pretty hearts, one pink and one red,
"Are bringing you love," the butterfly said.
"They tell you 'I love you' in a special way:
"With lots of love — Happy Valentine's Day!"
(Hint: This poem also makes a nice valentine for children to give their parents.)

The Valentine Box

Pretty colored paper, hearts and cupids too.
I made a box, with a hole on top,
To slip the valentines through.
I put valentines in all the boxes;
Making them was fun. . .
But when Valentine's Day was over,
My box had just one!

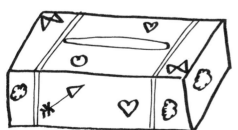

Five Lucky Leprechauns

The first one said, "I like green!" (thumb)
The second said, "I know what you mean!" (index)
The third one said, "I like gold!" (middle)
The fourth one said, "Gold's nice, I'm told." (ring)
The fifth one said, "Let's run away!" (pinky)
And they all disappeared on St. Patrick's Day!

Wearing of the Green

Michael's wearing a green shirt.
Terry's wearing a green skirt.
Lee's wearing a big green bow.
Kevin's wearing green pants, you know.
But look at Pat: not one green spot!
Guess what day Patrick forgot?

Leprechaun Footprints

We spied their footprints in our halls:
They'd left them on the ceilings,
They'd left them on the walls.

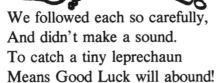

We followed each so carefully,
And didn't make a sound.
To catch a tiny leprechaun
Means Good Luck will abound!

Their footprints led us everywhere,
But not one did we see.
They're a cunning, crafty bunch,
Not caught so easily.

And then we saw a rainbow,
Oh so far away,
And the sign they'd left behind:
"Happy St. Patrick's Day!"

(Hint: Have a Leprechaun Treasure Hunt.
Cut small green footprints and tape them around the
school for the children to follow.)

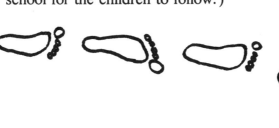

Five Little Leprechauns

This one has a beard of red;   (thumb)
This one likes to eat green bread.   (index)
This one likes to play bad tricks.   (middle)
This one tells you jokes for kicks.   (ring)
This one guards the gold, they say;   (pinky)
And they all wish you luck on St. Patrick's Day!

Paddy O. McLeprechaun

Paddy O. McLeprechaun was a funny man.
Paddy O. McLeprechaun lived in an old tin can.
Paddy O. McLeprechaun ate nothing but green candy.
Paddy O. McLeprechaun thought life was really dandy.
Paddy O. McLeprechaun then got a stomachache.
Paddy O. McLeprechaun drank a shamrock shake.
Paddy O. McLeprechaun is well and very old.
Paddy O. McLeprechaun just loves his pot of gold!

Sham rock
Shake

(Hint: Mix vanillla ice cream, milk and green
food coloring in the blender and you'll have
a shamrock shake!)

April Fool!

A day for playing tricks on
Everyone at school.
The only day it's safe to call
Your teacher "April Fool!"

Six Easter Eggs

The Easter Bunny said,
"These eggs are for you.
I hope you like red, yellow, and blue.
The spotted one is just delicious;
The marshmallow one is so nutritious!
And the last you'll really like a lot:
It's filled with the finest choc-o-late!"

Looking for Eggs

One egg, two eggs, three eggs, four —
Looks like I just found one more!
Five eggs in my basket, so beautiful to see;
Five eggs in my basket, count them now with me:
one — two — three — four — five!

Hunting Eggs

We hunted in the bushes,
Where stickers scratched our legs;
We overturned each garden stone,
As we hunted Easter eggs.

We filled up all our baskets —
It certainly was fun;
And yet I know next summer
We'll discover we missed one!

Little Chick, Little Bunny

Little Chick met Little Bunny
   One sunny Easter morn.
Said Little Chick to Little Bunny,
   "Come and share my corn."
Said Little Bunny to Little Chick,
   That happy Easter Day,
"Bunnies just eat carrots, Silly!"
   And then he hopped away.

From the Easter Bunny

The Bunny left a surprise for everyone to see:
A pretty china pink egg he left for Ann Marie;
A chocolate covered filled egg he left just for my dad;
And a stuffed pink Easter Bunny he left for little Brad.
Then he wanted a special gift, not one that was silly,
So for my mom, he left the best:
A lovely Easter lily.

Bunny Ears

Long ago and far away,
Lived the first Easter Bunny.

In a land so rich and green,
With days long, warm, and sunny.

But this Easter Bunny had ears
That were so small

That with these ears our bunny
Could scarcely hear at all.

Then on that first bright Easter
The bunny found such joy

By delivering a basket
To every girl and boy.

He wished to hear their laughter,
And so his ears they grew.

Now he hears their happiness
On Easter and all year through!

Easter Worm

Did you ever wonder,
    Wouldn't it be funny,
If we had an Easter Worm
    Instead of an Easter Bunny?

He couldn't hop around your house;
    He'd creep along the land.
And as for decorating eggs,
    He'd surely need a hand!

He could never be as cute
    As our dear Easter Bunny.
But if we had an Easter Worm
    Wouldn't it be funny?

Easter Clothes

Lee Anne has an Easter dress,
It's pretty pastel blues.
Christopher has a new suit,
A tie, and Easter shoes.
Mama has an Easter hat,
With flowers on the top;
And a matching coat and vest
Make an Easter suit for Pop!

Mother's Day

There shouldn't be a Mother's Day:
   It's just one day per year.
We need to tell her *every* day
   Just why she's very dear!

Father's Day

Who used to bounce me on his knee?
Who built me a house 'way up in a tree?
Who always gave his love to me?
   My Daddy!

Who always tucked me in at night?
Who made bad days turn out all right?
Who taught me how to fly my kite?
   My Daddy!

Flag Day

What do the stars and stripes mean?
A field of blue, now why?
I may not know,
But I'll stand proud
When my flag is passing by.

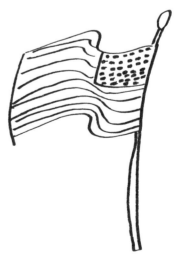

Our Flag

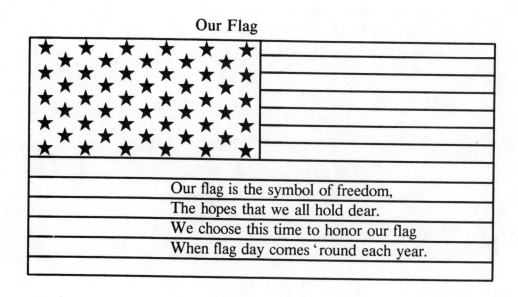

Our flag is the symbol of freedom,
The hopes that we all hold dear.
We choose this time to honor our flag
When flag day comes 'round each year.

July the Fourth

Picnics, fireworks, sparklers and noise:
July the Fourth is fun for all girls and boys.

Parades and bands, hot apple pie.
For Freedom we celebrate the Fourth of July.

Arbor Day

For their shade and the ways they please
We choose this day to honor trees.

And for their ageless history
Upon this day we'll plant a tree.

Ghosts

The first ghost said, "How do you do?" (thumb)
The second ghost said, "How do you Boo?" (index)
The third ghost said, "I feel all right." (middle)
The fourth ghost said, "I'm dressed in white." (ring)
The fifth ghost said, "I like to scream!" (pinky)
And they all went a-haunting on Hallowe'en.

Ghostly Goodies

What do ghosts like to eat the most?
Why, for breakfast it's GHOST TOAST!

The Haunted House

Cracked and broken windows,
Barred and creaking doors;
Holes in the ceilings,
Trap doors in the floors.
Faces in the mirrors
That are not my own.
Ghosts and witches call this
"Home Sweet Haunted Home."

The Ghost Family

Pappa Ghost said, "Boo!"
Mamma Ghost said, "Boo!" too.
But Baby Ghost said, "Boo Hoo! Hoo!"

Witches's Brew

Stir and mix, (stirring motion with large spoon)
Mix and stir,
Until it's bubbly hot!
Throw some scary things into—
Into the Hallowe'en pot!
(Hint: Children stand in a circle around the
make-believe Hallowe'en pot. Each child takes
a turn telling what he'd throw into the pot: bat,
bones, snakes, etc.)

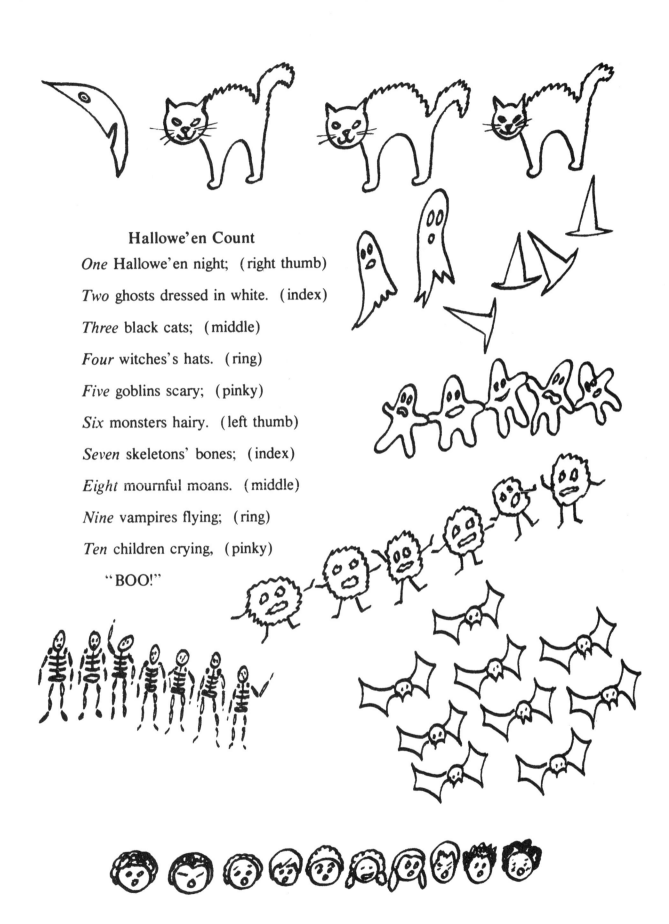

Hallowe'en Count

One Hallowe'en night; (right thumb)

Two ghosts dressed in white. (index)

Three black cats; (middle)

Four witches's hats. (ring)

Five goblins scary; (pinky)

Six monsters hairy. (left thumb)

Seven skeletons' bones; (index)

Eight mournful moans. (middle)

Nine vampires flying; (ring)

Ten children crying, (pinky)

    "BOO!"

135

The Hallowe'en Wedding

Billy Ghost and Willa Witch became bride and groom.
Billy flew up to the church and Willa rode her broom.
The preacher asked the couple each to say, I do."
Willa laughed, "Heh! Heh! Heh!" and Billy Ghost yelled, "Boo!"
"I now pronounce you Ghost and Witch!" and everybody cheered.
And when the wedding was all over
The happy couple disappeared!

Hallowe'en Colors

Pumpkins and cats;
Tall witches' hats'
Hallowe'en colors:
Orange and black.

Hallowe'en

This is my pumpkin, round and fat; (make circle with hand)
Here is the point of a witches' hat. (index fingers touch)
Here is the mouth of a ghost who says, "Boo!" (thumb and index finger touch)
And here are his eyes that are staring at you! (make circles with both hands over eyes)

Five Fat Turkeys

Five fat turkeys all in a row. (show five fingers)
The first one said, "Where shall we go?" (thumb)
The second one said, "I really don't care." (index)
The third one said, "I smell dinner in the air." (middle)
The fourth one said, "Thanksgiving Day is fun!" (ring)
The fifth one said, "Thanksgiving? Let's run!" (pinky)
Then "Whoooo!" went the wind,
And "Swish!" went the snow,
And five fat turkeys ran off in a row! (hand behind back)

Mr. Turkey

Here is Mr. Turkey with his tail feathers high.
Gobble, Mr. Turkey, now fly! fly! fly! (move hand over head)

Soon it will be Thanksgiving Day:
Time for Mr. Turkey to run away! (hand moves behind back)

The First Thanksgiving

This is the sun on that first Thanksgiving Day. (hands in circle over head)

This is the way the Pilgrims pray. (hands in prayer)

These are the Indians proud and strong; (arms folded on chest)

And this is the end of my Thanksgiving song.

The Pilgrim Family

Here's the Pilgrim Father, good and strong and tall; (thumb)
Here's the Pilgrim Mother, who takes care of them all. (index)
Here's the Pilgrim Sister, who helps to cook and sew; (middle)
Here's the Pilgrim Brother, who makes the tall corn grow. (ring)
Here's the Pilgrim Baby; we'll soon teach him to pray; (ring)
This is the Pilgrim Family, together on Thanksgiving Day.

The Helpful Indians

The Indians helped the Pilgrims
Their precious seeds to sow.
The Indians helped the Pilgrims
Make their tall corn grow.
The Indians helped the Pilgrims
Hunt food on their own.
The Indians helped the Pilgrims
Make America their home.

138

I Am Thankful

"I am thankful," said the cat, "for my hearth so warm."
"I am thankful," said the farmer, "for my big red barn."
"I am thankful," said the bird, "for my nest high in the tree."
"I am thankful," said the fish, "for my friends deep in the sea."
"I am thankful," said the duck, "for my lake so blue."
"I am thankful," said the Father, "thankful, my child, for you."

Thanksgiving Feast

Apple pie and dumplings, potatoes piled high;
Busy in the kitchen, Thanksgiving Day is nigh.
Crisp, brown, juicy turkey, stuffing piping hot;
Fresh bread in the oven, vegetables in the pot.
Everything is ready, company at the door.
Take a minute now and think:
What are you thankful for?

Manners

Let us try to be polite,
In all we say and do.
Remember now, those special words:
"Excuse me," "Please," and "Thank you".

Our Thanksgiving Table

We're all around the table,
Mom and Dad and me,
Counting all our blessings,
For home and family.

My Turkey

Look at my turkey's feathers —   (hold up five fingers)
   Yellow (thumb)
   Brown (index)
   Red (ring)
Here is my turkey's sturdy beak,
Right here on his head.
And what does my turkey say,
Every day and every night?
Why, "Gobble! Gobble! Gobble!"
He says it till it's right! (wiggle all five fingers)

The Drumstick

Dad carves up the turkey and slices it on the plate,
And when he cuts the drumstick, I can hardly wait!
The grownups all love turkey, and they can have the rest,
But they'll never get a drumstick —
That's the part kids love the best!

The Wishbone

Mommy got the wishbone,
She'll make a wish with me.
If I get the longest end,
What will my wish bring me?
(Hint: Bring a wishbone to class and encourage
the children to share their wishes with you.)

My Menorah

Candles brightly shining, light one every night.
And when all seven are glowing,
My Menorah looks just right!

The Menorah

Seven colored candles, red and
Yellow and blue.
The Shamus is the Helper —
It lights each one for you.
The Menorah tells of a miracle
That happened long ago.
At Hanukkah we celebrate
As we watch the candles glow.

The Dreidyl

Spin my shiny Dreidyl, a lucky "shin" for me.

Spin my shiny Dreidyl, a winner I will be.

Spin my shiny Dreidyl, Hanukkah "gelt" my prize;

Spin my shiny Dreidyl, before I close my eyes.

The Eight Nights of Hanukkah

Count the nights of Hanukkah:
  Two, four, six and eight.
We light another candle,
  That's how we celebrate.

And on each night a gift received,
  Some large ones and some small.
Fun and time with family,
  Special love shared by all.

Potato Latkes

Hanukkah treats are latkes;
We fry them in a pan.
I can eat more latkes
Than almost anyone can!

Christmas Symbols

Here's our pretty Christmas tree, with presents underneath.

(hands point upward over head)

Here's a colored ornament. (thumb and index form circle)

And here's a Christmas wreath. (two hands for circle over head)

Here's the old brick chimney, (stand with arms straight up)

With Santa coming through. (stoop down)

And here's a Christmas message:

"Happy Holidays to you!" (point)

Christmas Trees

Christmas trees! Christmas trees!
How many do you see?
Christmas trees! Christmas trees!
Count them with me.
A tall one, (thumb)
A short one, (index)
And one that's so fine — (middle)
One of those three will surely be mine!

The Star

I made a pretty star today, to top my Christmas tree;
With silver, gold, and glitter, it's as shiny as can be.
And when I place it on the top,
Dad says it looks just fine.
Although it's not a store bought one,
He loves it 'cause it's mine!

Stocking by the Fireplace

Stockings by the fireplace,
For Mom and Dad and me.
Stockings by the fireplace,
Count them: one, two, three.
Daddy's is the biggest;
Mom's is trimmed with lace.
And *mine* you'll know
By the hole in the toe —
Three stockings by the fireplace!

The Stocking

What's inside your stocking?
Candy and a ball.
What's inside your stocking?
A shiny penny, that's not all!
So many small surprises
Inside my stocking rest:
Of all my Christmas presents
I love my stocking best!

Santa Claus

Here are Santa's rosy cheeks; (touch cheeks)
Here is Santa's nose. (touch nose)
Here is Santa's moustache; (make pretend moustache)
Here are Santa's clothes. (touch clothes)
Here is Santa's snow white beard; (make pretend beard)
Here is Santa's sleigh. (pretend to hold reins)
Hurry now to catch a look,
Before he flies away!

The Real Santa

Santas on the street corner
Santas in the stores.
Santas in the windows,
Santas at the doors.

So many different Santas—
They're everywhere, I see.
How will I know on Christmas if
The real Santa visited me?

Santa's Toy Shop

This elf makes electric trains; (right thumb)
This elf stripes the candy canes. (right index)
This elf makes baby dolls that talk; (right middle)
This elf makes brown bears that walk. (right ring)
This elf makes bikes and boats; (right pinky)
This elf makes warm winter coats. (left thumb)
This elf makes gifts for Mom and Dad; (left index)
This elf checks who's good and bad. (left middle)
This elf makes electronic games; (left pinky)
This elf wraps and writes our names. (left pinky)
All the elves pack up Santa's sleigh,
Ready for us (point to self) on Christmas Day!

What If. . . .

What if Santa's reindeer
On Christmas went on strike?
Would Viola get her dolly?
Would I get my bike?

What would Santa do then,
Without his eight reindeer?
I suppose my Merry Christmas
Would be postponed a *year*!

Santa's Reindeer

This reindeer maps out the way; (thumb)

This reindeer heads up the sleigh. (index)

This reindeer's nose lights up the sky; (middle)

This reindeer helps the team fly high. (ring)

This reindeer helps when there's no snow; (pinky)

This reindeer knows just where to go. (thumb)

This reindeer watches all the toys; (index)

This reindeer checks off girls and boys. (middle)

Hurry, Everyone! Santa's late!

Count the reindeer: 2, 4, 6, 8!

Going Home

It's time to put your things away;
Our day is at an end.
You may get in line now:
Stand beside a friend.

Tomorrow is another day;
I'll see you all right here.
Our school day now is over,
Give a happy cheer:

   HOORAY!